A SPIRIT DAUGHTER
WORKBOOK

---

written by
Jill Wintersteen

FOR THE LIBRA SEASON

+

THE NEW MOON
Saturday, September 28th, 2019
11:36AM PDT

This Workbook is designed to be used throughout the Season of Libra and during her New Moon. Use pages 2-15 + 30-33 to help you align with the Seasonal Sun Energy of Libra, which begins September 23rd and ends October 22nd. Use pages 16-29 during the days around the Libra New Moon, September 28th, to harness her power to create a new reality.

LIBRA

Libra more than any other sign in the zodiac understands the meaning of the word TEAM. The energy of Libra governs all of our partnerships. She teaches us that all relationships require teamwork to thrive, grow, and stand the test of time. According to Libra, true partnership is formed when there is empathy, vulnerability, and the willingness to see each other's perspectives. To achieve these things, though, we must first understand ourselves and what creates our own internal peace. The Season of Libra is about first understanding our center, then learning how to step away from our center to walk in someone else's shoes. Libra shows us that unless we have inner balance, we cannot take on a differing viewpoint for fear of losing our self. It is only after we master our own energy and emotions that we can empathize with another.

The scales represent Libra in the zodiac. Her sign is a constant reminder that balance takes effort. Her season can bring up chaos in our world to give us the opportunity to find balance. Harmony often cannot be understood and created until disharmony is experienced. We cannot learn what tools calm us down and stabilize our emotions if we never feel instability. Aligning with Libra does not mean suppressing or ignoring your emotions. It means quite the opposite. True embodiment of the Libra vibration asks you to feel deeply into your emotions to understand them and learn their pattern. Only then can you bring peace to your emotional body at any time. Life isn't perfect, and things happen, which cause reactions. It's quite normal to feel anger, sadness, joy, and the myriad of other emotions we humans are capable of feeling. The key, though, is to understand what makes you tick, what pushes your buttons and what kind of reactions you are prone to making. Then you can develop tools which help you either become aware of your emotions without reacting to them or return quickly to emotional equilibrium in the event you do become unbalanced. Libra's real end game? To help us remain calm in any situation while fully experiencing our emotions.

Once you understand how to maintain inner peace, you can embrace Libra's next opportunity which is to become a better teammate. We live in a world with other people. Our daily life includes a variety of relationships with these people. We exchange energy with others; we help one another, we share responsibilities, we enjoy and experience life together. Successfully navigated, each of our relationships takes awareness from both parties and the willingness to be vulnerable. Emotional vulnerability is when we let down our guards, show our true feelings, and risk being hurt or rejected because of our honesty. There is uncertainty and some discomfort, but there is also great rewards. When we allow ourselves to be fully seen, we cultivate love, compassion, true belonging, and empathy. We can learn genuine empathy for others, which is what helps us remain in partnerships even when we don't agree with one another.

Throughout Libra Season, first, work on yourself by cultivating your own inner harmony. Then begin to observe how you show up in your partnerships when you are calm versus when you are in a reactive state. Go even further with this observation by starting to understand how your inner peace affects your ability to empathize with someone else. When you feel emotionally calm, is it easier to be vulnerable? Furthermore, when you can be vulnerable, how does this affect your ability to communicate your perspective to another? Lastly, when you are in a state of inner harmony yourself, do you find it easier to empathize with another? Experiment with these concepts throughout Libra Season and invite your partners to join you as you grow together.

People with their Sun in Libra are the peacemakers of the zodiac. They often can understand several points of view at the same time. They empathize with those around them and strive to create equality wherever they go. Libras also understands the importance of embracing opposition. The whole can not exist without two halves, and Libra Suns are ok with extreme sides, as long as everyone is treated fairly.

People with their Moon in Libra tend to thrive in partnerships. They will not just accept any partner, though. They require true emotional understanding and the willingness to see their perspective. Libra Moon's crave balance in their lives and are continually striving to create harmony both in their internal and external world.

MOONSCOPES

Moonscopes are based on your Moon Sign. They provide guidance and insight about how your personal Moon, otherwise known as your emotions, will be affected by the Seasonal energy of Libra. These energies will amplify on her New Moon.

Aries Moon: You are fiercely independent both in and out of a relationship. You crave autonomy and the freedom to do your own thing. You need a partner who understands your need for some alone time, as well as one who will align with your spontaneous nature. You are attached to people who display courage and can keep up with your fast-paced mind and spirit.

Taurus Moon: You tend to like the slow lane in life. Not because you can't move quickly, but because moving slowly is just more enjoyable. You love to indulge in the finer things life has to offer: Sundays spent in fine linen sheets, long brunches filled with laughter, or late night picnics on the beach lit by candlelight. You need a partner who can enjoy life with all of their senses as you do. You also need someone who understands that you don't want to rush anything, including how you process emotions.

Gemini Moon: You like to talk it out. You have many thoughts and feelings running through your energy and need space to sort them out through communication. You crave a good listener and do well with partners who are willing to sit with you as you make order out of the chaos in your heart. You need a partner who keeps you on your toes with pleasant surprises and peaks your curiosity with their quick wit.

Cancer Moon: You love nourishment both for yourself and for others. You have a deep capacity to feel and understand your emotions. You need a partner who understands your need for self-care but who will also wade through the sea of feelings you often possess. You love to be at home and crave someone who enjoys days spent in the house filled with good food and maybe a long bubble bath. Cooking is a natural expression of your energy, so find someone who enjoys being cared for and appreciates you for your efforts.

Leo Moon: Your heart is big, and you need to express it. Authentic self-expression is what you crave, and you need partners who can be your loyal audience. You love both appreciation and praise, but more than anything you need space to be yourself. Play is also an essential part of your relationships, especially when things feel challenging. Find partners who can laugh with you and remember that life is meant to be enjoyed not taken so seriously.

Virgo Moon: You love order and structure, as they make you feel in control of your world. You crave a partner who appreciates your precision in life and who has their own world in order. Chaos is not your thing, and you don't want to spend your time organizing someone else's life for them. You do, however, love to serve. You are a doer and like to do things for your partner like cook a good meal or teach them one of your many life skill sets. Seek a partner who appreciates your knowledge and profound understanding of the technicalities in life.

*You can look up your Moon Sign at astrocharts.com

MOONSCOPES

Libra Moon: You crave harmony in every area of your life, including your relationships. You are not one for drama or game playing. You do like a partner who can keep up with you mentally and is capable of challenging you with a diplomatic debate. They must be able to listen intently to your argument and at the end of it, remember that each side has some truth in it. You also need peace and serenity in your surroundings. Pick a partner who appreciates your love of aesthetics and is willing to spend the day crafting the perfect sanctuary.

Scorpio Moon: You are emotionally intense, and this intensity isn't for everyone. You protect your heart fiercely, only allowing a few to peak into the depths of your inner world. You are on a constant quest to experience every emotion, transform them into knowledge, then evolve into the next version of yourself. You need a partner who will give you space to do your inner work while understanding the many shifts that take place in your emotions and energy.

Sagittarius Moon: You crave expansion. Expansion of your heart, of your mind, and your knowledge. You need partners who want to experience the world with you and embrace new cultures, people, and places. You have an optimistic heart and assume that everything with work out just as it should. Pick a partner who embraces this same type of faith and is willing to jump into the unknown with nothing but trust and a backpack.

Capricorn Moon: You crave control in your world and your heart. If you could place your emotions in a spreadsheet to keep them neat and tidy, you would. This organization is not a bad thing. You generally know what you want in life and how you feel about it. You need a partner who appreciates your well-controlled emotions and gives you space to sort them out on the rare occasions they do become chaotic. Choose a partner who is stable in their energy and can take care of themselves.

Aquarius Moon: You crave freedom in all ways, including the mind and the heart. This does not mean you're not a good partner; you just need room for independence and the freedom to redefine the terms of conventional partnerships. Choose partners who understand your need for uniqueness in all that you do as well as your love for humanity. You tend to feel with your mind and can overthink emotions. Embrace people who inspire you to be vulnerable every once in a while, and allow your emotions to take over.

Pisces Moon: You feel deeply, both your own emotions and the emotions of others. You are one with the world and need partners who understand that when they come into your life, they become one with our consciousness. You also need people who respect your boundaries, as they are hard for you to maintain. Most of all though, you need someone who will spend hours in a dream state with you, experiencing the world for what it is and soaking up the true essence of nature as your imaginations merge into a state of bliss.

*You can look up your Moon Sign at astrocharts.com

CRYSTALS FOR LIBRA

Lapis Lazuli is a magical stone that connects to the element of Air. It stimulates both wisdom and peace simultaneously, activating your highest visions. Lapis has the power to reveal the whole picture of any situation and brings a clear perspective. It is also a stone of truth and will allow you to see the truth of any partnership while dispelling any negative thoughts. Lapis is perfect for both meditating and negotiating. Hold a piece if you need wisdom at any point throughout your day and have some while you have heartfelt conversations with loved ones. It will facilitate healing on all levels, including creating a bridge for restorative conversations. Lapis is deep purple with gold flecks.

Lapis Lazuli vibrates to the mantra: "I am at peace."

Ruby Tourmaline is a stone of the heart. It helps dispel negative emotions of guilt, shame and depression, and call in energies of love and compassion. It also helps to balance the right and left hemisphere of the brain, combining both masculine and feminine energies. Tourmaline will also bring about the feeling of peace by balancing the energetic body. Hold some while meditating if you need to find a middle ground in your emotions, or energy. It will help you call in harmonious vibrations ready to return you to an equanimous mind. Ruby Tourmaline is burgundy and white.

Ruby Tourmaline vibrates with the mantra: "I am balanced."

Ametrine is a combination of amethyst and citrine. It's a very energetic stone and can provide a spark to the mind and spirit, helping to cultivate new creativity. It will help you realize your dreams while giving the energy to manifest them. Ametrine also helps dispel negativity, and call in the energy of optimism and positive thinking. It's an excellent stone to have while setting intentions, dreaming, and finding new ways to express yourself. Ametrine also helps integrate masculine and feminine energy and is wonderful to use when creating harmony amongst these vibrations. Hold some while meditating, or wear some in the form of jewelry to fuse together energies for creation. Ametrine is purple and yellow.

Ametrine vibrates to the mantra: "I am connected."

Lepidolite is known as a stone of transition. It helps ease anxiety and restlessness when transitioning from one version of ourselves to another. It can help with any life transition, as well, such as a career shift, a move to another home, or even when transitioning into a new partnership. If change is on the horizon for you, hold a piece as you meditate, to help return you to your center during turbulent times. Lepidolite is gray/purple.

Lepidolite vibrates to the mantra: "I am centered."

Girasol Opal is a gentle stone which can activate your capacity to mirror another emotionally. This mirroring is particularly useful when communicating with partners to cultivate empathy and understanding. Hold a piece in your hand while speaking with another to see the world from their perspective. It will also help you communicate more freely and speak your mind, mirroring your own energy to another. The energies of Girasol Opal will also guide you to the truth of any issue, making it easier to resolve a conflict between you and another. Use it to calm your mind when confusion has arisen. It will create peace and clarity within you and your partners. Girasol Opal is milky in color.

Girasol Opal vibrates to the mantra: "I project truth."

LIBRA LUNAR FLOW

Balance in our energetic body is a reflection of balance in our physical and mental bodies. If we want to maintain equanimity in our entire system, it's important to practice a discipline like yoga, which cultivates harmony in the physical body. Through linking breath and movement, yoga integrates our mind, body, and spirit, making a perfect tool to help us cultivate inner peace and harmony. Yoga also helps integrate both sides of our physical body; right and left. The left side represents our feminine, receptive, side, while the right represents our masculine, doing, side. Often we have discrepancies in how we use each side of our body, favoring one over the other. We also tend to injure one side more due to imbalances in musculature and dependency. The following sequence is designed to bring harmony to your energy and balance to your entire system. Practice it throughout the season of Libra and on her New Moon. Try to alternate which side you begin with each time you practice, starting on the right one day for each pose, then on the left the next. When we consciously switch our dominant side, we recalibrate our dependency on one side of the body.

Seated Twist
Begin in a crossed legged position on your mat. You may sit on a block or a bolster to elevate your hips. Close your eyes as you take five breaths, counting up to four on each inhale and back down on each exhale. Allow this breath to set the pace for the rest of the practice. Open your eyes. Inhale, reach your arms to the sky, exhale twist to the right, placing your left hand on your right knee and your right hand behind you for a twist. Look over your right shoulder to extend the twist into your neck. Feel your entire spine rotating as your hips stay grounded and centered. Take 5 breaths here, then release. Switch the cross of your legs and repeat on the other side.

Cat/Cow
Come to hands and knees. Inhale, arch through your back gazing at the ceiling > Exhale, curl through your spine gazing at the belly button. Repeat for 5 breaths > Downward Facing Dog for 5 breaths > Walk hands back to feet to a Forward Bend for 5 breaths > roll slowly up to standing.

Sun Salutation A // 3 Rounds
Stand at the top of your mat. Inhale stretch your arms overhead > Exhale fold forward > Inhale lengthen out your back > Exhale step back to plank pose and lower to the ground > Inhale reach your chest up for cobra pose, legs on the ground > Exhale to Downward Dog Pose. Stay here for 5 breaths and feel your entire body expand. On Exhale, step to the top of the mat > Inhale lengthen through your spine > Exhale fold forward > Inhale come up to standing, reaching arms overhead. > Exhale hands to your heart. Pause for a moment and feel yourself centered throughout your body. Repeat two more times.

LIBRA LUNAR FLOW

Windmill

Step your feet 3-4ft apart. Exhale fold forward over your legs, lowering hands to the ground or a block. Inhale lengthen out through your spine making it parallel to the ground > Exhale > Inhale lift your left arm to the ceiling, twisting to the left. Exhale lower the arm > Inhale lift your right arm, twisting to the right. Exhale lower the arm. This is one round, repeat four times, moving with the breath.

Crescent Pose with Twist

Bring your feet back together at the top of your mat. Inhale lift your arms overhead > Exhale fold forward. Inhale lengthen out through your back > Exhale step your right foot back keeping the knee off the floor. Place your right hand under the right shoulder and twist to the left, lifting the left arm towards the sky for an easy twist. Breathe deeply into your rib cage for 5 breaths then release into plank pose. Lower to the ground for Cobra > Exhale to Downward Dog. Take 5 breaths > step the right foot forward, for a Crescent Twist. 5 breaths on this side > step to the front of the mat > Forward Fold. Take 5 deep breaths here as your spine unravels. Inhale slowly round up to standing, feeling spacious in your front and back body.

Warrior 1 > Side Stretch > Twisted Triangle

Standing at the top of your mat, Inhale lift your arms up > Exhale into Chair Pose > Inhale > Exhale fold forward > Inhale lengthen through your spine > Exhale plank pose into chaturanga (elbows bent) > Inhale into Upward Facing Dog (chest lifts, hands and tops of the feet stay on the ground) > Exhale Downward Facing Dog > Inhale step the left foot forward for Warrior 1, back foot remains flat, turning in at a 60 degree angle. Bend into the front knee and lift the arms. Remain here for 5 breaths, lengthening your torso. Exhale lower your arms to the ground and hop the back foot in 1ft > Inhale lengthen your spine as you straighten your front leg > Exhale fold over your front leg. If your hamstrings are tight, use blocks under your hands. Breathe here for 5 breaths, lengthen through the spine on each inhale and fold deeper on each exhale. Inhale lengthen, place the right hand on a block about twelve inches inside your left foot > Exhale rotate your spine to the left, lifting the left arm to the sky. Keep the hips level and feel your body rotating around the central axis of your spine. Take 5 breaths. Release both hands to the ground stepping back into Plank Pose > Exhale chaturanga > Inhale Upward Dog > Exhale Downward Dog. Repeat on the right side, ending back at Downward Dog.

Supported Bridge Pose > 5 mins

Grab a block and lay down on your back. Bend your knees and place your feet hips width apart. Press down through your feet as you lift the hips for Bridge Pose. Place the block on any comfortable height and allow it to support your hips. Close your eyes and deepen your breath. Allow all of your thoughts to dissolve as you relax into the block, feeling entirely supported and at peace. Spend 5 minutes here then slowly release down through the spine as you lower the hips back to the mat. Gently squeeze your knees towards your chest and make small circles on your sacrum. Breathe into your lower back, filling it with energy and air.

Spinal Twist

Laying on your back. Hug the left knee into your chest and send it over the right side for a spinal twist. Reach your left arm out to the side, stretching through the chest. Take 5 breaths here, then switch sides. On each Inhale, feel your back lengthen, on each exhale twist a little deeper.

Savasana

Stretch both your legs out long on the mat and place your palms facing upward in a receptive motion. Feel your entire body supported by the ground beneath you. Let your breath become natural and feel the energy circulating through you from your practice.

LIBRA MEDITATION

There are many tools available for us to create calm and peace in our energetic body. Libra is an air sign and reminds us that our breath, and the way we are breathing, helps create equanimity in our energetic field. Breathwork is your first tool in maintaining energetic balance. It is always available to you and can be used no matter where you are or what you are doing. The breath is also a clue to when our inner equilibrium is disturbed or is on the verge of being disturbed. You may notice when you are feeling unbalanced emotionally, your breathing becomes shallow or you may even hold your breath. Libra reminds us that maintaining balance is also a focus of catching ourselves before the imbalance occurs. The breath can help us keep ourselves calm at the moment when we are about to react or become unstable in our emotions. Work with your breathing throughout Libra Season, experimenting with different types of breathing to find the one that restores harmony within you.

Alternating Nostril Breathing

This practice is a yogic breath work that balances the right and left sides, bringing equanimity to the energetic body. Begin in a comfortable seated position with your spine upright. Using your right hand, place your thumb on your right nostril and your ring finger on your left nostril. The index and middle finger will rest on your forehead. You can also hold your right elbow with your left hand for support. Close your eyes. Begin by closing your right nostril and breathing only through your left for a count of four. Hold both sides and your breath for a count of four, then hold your left nostril exhaling only through the right for a count of four. Then reverse it. Breathe in through the right, hold, then exhale through the left- all for a count of 4. This is one complete round. Complete eight full rounds. When you are finished, release your hand and sit, observing the equality of the breath.

Breath Meditation

Meditation is another tool to help us maintain internal harmony and peace. When we cultivate a daily meditation practice, we train our mind to be nonreactive, helping us throughout the day to remain equanimous in the face of challenges. Throughout Libra Season try meditating for at least five minutes each morning. Extend this time to eleven or fifteen minutes when you feel comfortable. Below is a simple breath meditation which can give your mind something to focus on instead of your thoughts.

You can perform this meditation seated or laying down. In this practice, you are just observing the breath without changing it at all. Focus all your attention on the tip of the nose, where you can feel the breath coming in and out. Even if you can't feel the breath, keep your attention here, and your senses will eventually sharpen. Just observe the feeling of the inhale and exhale. Suspend judgment on the quality of the breath, and just let it be. If your mind wanders, gently bring it back to the breath with compassion. Do this as many times as needed. Do not try to fight the thoughts, redirect the attention back to the breath. Feel the flow of the breath at the tip of the nose, as if this is the only part of you that exists in this moment.

Partner Gazing Meditation

This meditation is done with another person. This can be anyone; a loved one, a co-worker, or even a stranger. Sit down in a comfortable position across from your partner. Sit fairly close, but you do not need to touch. Set a timer for three minutes. Begin by staring into your partner's eyes. Try not to look away for the entire time. This can be intense, and that's ok. It may bring a smile to your face or a tear to your eye. Whatever occurs, continue to stare into your partner's eyes. As you gaze, sync your breath with your partner's. Observe what you feel when you are fully seen by one another. Once you are finished, you may choose to share your experience with your partner. What did you feel? Was it uncomfortable? Practice this meditation often with your close partners to help align the natural rhythms of your body, opening up a pathway for better communication and more healing exchanges.

ALIGNING the SPIRIT

8 Tips for Cultivating Balanced Relationships

once you master your internal seas,

no wave can ever throw you off balance.

- spirit daughter

Communicate
Communication is the key to any partnership, romantic or otherwise. Make sure your communication is always clear, concise, and kind between you and your partners. Speak your mind when you need to, but also respect your partner's space. If a conflict arises, set a time for you to speak about it when both of you can focus entirely on the problem. Never catch your partner off guard when there is an important topic to be discussed. When communicating, remember to listen as much as you speak. If you feel you need a break, take it and return to the topic at a later time.

Manage Expectations
Often we develop unrealistic expectations of our partners. Furthermore, they often don't know we have these expectations. Begin by understanding what you may be expecting from your partner and be realistic in their ability to deliver what you're asking. Also, make sure to communicate your expectations to free both of you from the burden of having to read minds. Create clear guidelines on what each of you is responsible for in the partnership and steer away from idealized expectations of what each of you can contribute.

Be Appreciative
Appreciate your partners! Tell them every day how grateful you are for the ways they make your world a better place. This is a simple activity but often overlooked, especially with our closest partners. Set an intention to tell the people in your life why you appreciate them daily.

ALIGNING the SPIRIT

Be You

It can be so easy to lose ourselves in partnerships. We take on other people's energy, and it can be hard to distinguish what is ours and what is another's. This enmeshment is heightened when we live with people or communicate with them on a daily basis. Remember to take time to return to yourself. New Moons are excellent times to do this. Reconnect with who YOU are at your core, and your relationships will be better off for it.

Grow Together

People who cannot grow together, unfortunately, grow apart. We are continually changing, expanding, and evolving. As the years pass, we change- and that's a good thing! Our priorities shift, and our life follows. Long lasting relationships must be flexible and capable of changing as each partner shifts into different versions of themselves. Find ways to support your partners' growth, and for them to support yours. Discuss your evolving self and create ways to make the partnership capable of shifting as each of you grows.

Compromise

Part of the joy of partnerships is we have someone to share our experiences and life. The trade-off for this is we can't always do exactly what we want when we want to do it. There are many things we still can do, but there are times when we need to meet our partner halfway and compromise. To make true compromise work without resentment, first, know what is important to you and what you can let go if needed. Learn when to stand your ground and fight for your priorities, and when to shift to meet your partner. In essence, pick your battles wisely, what isn't of utmost importance to you, give up for the sake of the relationship.

Empathize

Libra is all about harmony: learn to create it in every partnership through empathy. Always remember when dealing with another person, they are different than you. They have different perspectives, different energy, and a different life path. Make an effort to understand their viewpoint and help them understand yours. This is especially important in the face of conflict. Always ask yourself how your partner may see a situation differently than you. This does not mean one of has to be right or wrong; it just means you are both human.

Make Time

We are often so busy we can barely make time for ourselves, let alone our partnerships. They need nourishment, though, and time for re-bonding. Carve out space in your schedule to give attention to your relationships. This can be a date night with your partner, or lunch with a good friend; it can even be a phone call if you are not in the same city. Show your partners they are important to you by making time to nurture the relationship.

FALL EQUINOX

SEPT 23RD

The Fall Equinox ushers in a time of release, when nature herself lets go of the old to prepare for the new. Align with the energy of this day and the start of Libra by releasing anything which disturbs your inner balance. Know that as you release this energy, you are transforming it, much like when the trees let go of their leaves, they become part of the Earth again. In the space below, first write what you are releasing this Fall. In the second column, write what you are transforming this energy into over the next three months. Hold the intention of this release bringing equanimity to your energy and your life.

I AM RELEASING   BY TRANSFORMING IT INTO

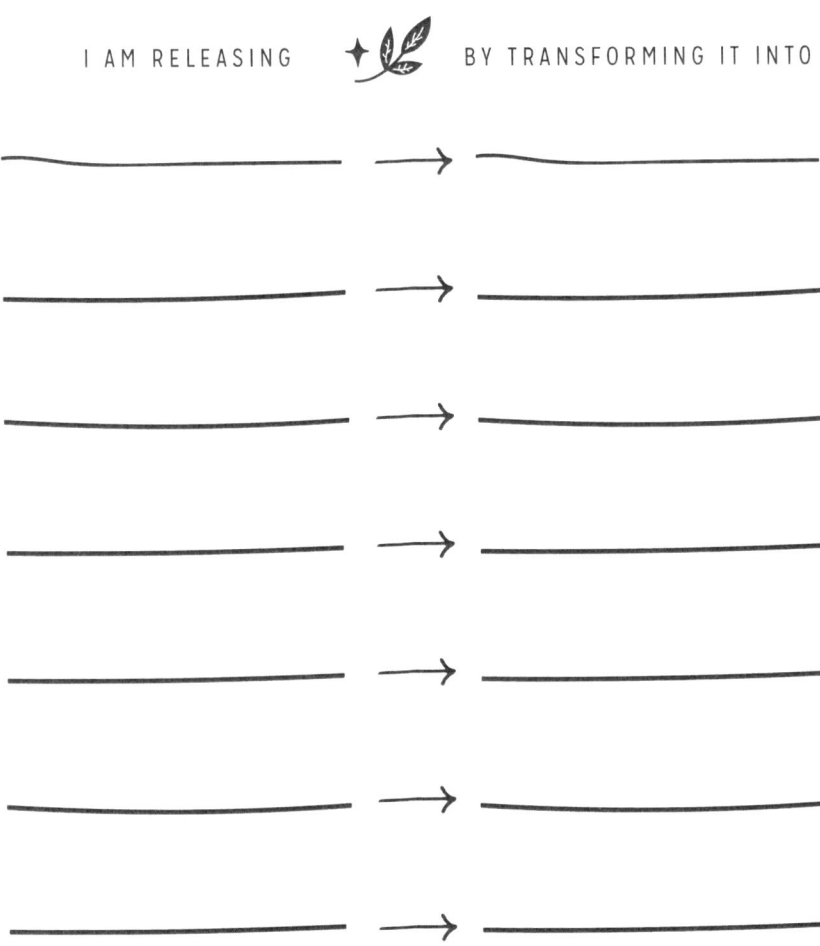

WANING MOON

SEPT 24TH - SEPT 27TH

As the Moon continues to Wane, revisit your intentions from last month and possibly the month before. Which ones do you want to continue to nourish and which ones do you want to shift to make space for new intentions on the New Moon?

I AM CONTINUING
TO WORK ON THESE
INTENTIONS OVER THE
NEXT LUNAR CYCLE:

I AM LETTING GO OF
THESE INTENTIONS
TO MAKE SPACE FOR
NEW ONES:

NEW MOON

SEPT 28TH

LIBRA IN..	FOCUS ON...
1ST HOUSE	self, your identity and how you project yourself into the world.
2ND HOUSE	self-worth, your feelings about your resources and your possessions.
3RD HOUSE	communications and how you exchange energy.
4TH HOUSE	home and how you nourish yourself.
5TH HOUSE	how you enjoy life and what restores your heart's joy.
6TH HOUSE	how you offer your gifts to the world through service.
7TH HOUSE	your relationships and partnerships.
8TH HOUSE	your personal growth and transformation.
9TH HOUSE	how you obtain knowledge and respond to adventure.
10TH HOUSE	your career.
11TH HOUSE	what you are contributing to humanity.
12TH HOUSE	your spirituality and spiritual growth.

NEW MOON

SEPT 28TH

New Moons are powerful days when we have the opportunity to experience the combined energy of the Sun and the Moon. The Sun remains in a zodiac constellation for four weeks, making its way slowly through all twelve signs within a year. Your Sun sign, the one you probably identify with the most, is the sign where the Sun was positioned when you were born. When the Sun is in a sign, it takes on those vibrations and influences our energetic system. Being born with those frequencies in the air infuses them into the core of your personality. Every year, the Sun returns to the place you were born, and you experience a Solar Return, otherwise known as your birthday. Throughout your Sun Season, you'll feel a heightened sense of your personality and are given the opportunity to return to your home frequency, the center of your being. If you are a Libra, then this is your season, and you'll feel even more Libra-like than usual. If you're not a Libra, then you'll still feel the effects of Libra's vibration and can align with them to enhance your relationships, harmony, and sense of balance. No matter your sign, the Sun is still in Libra for all us, and we each can tap into Libra's frequency.

The Moon moves more quickly than the Sun. She travels through all twelve zodiacs every 29.5 days. For 2.5 days of her Lunar Cycle, she meets the Sun in the same zodiac, and we are graced with a New Moon. Just like a Sun sign, you also have a Moon sign. This sign was the position of the Moon when you were born. The Moon governs your emotional body and guides you to what you need for fulfillment in your life. Your Moon sign is a significant part of your constitution for it governs how you FEEL. When the Moon returns to the place it was when you were born, you experience a Moon return. This event happens every month at some point for each of us. Over this period, you'll often experience intense emotions and heightened intuition. When the New Moon occurs in your Moon sign, you'll be given an opportunity to create a new pattern of emotional and even behavioral reactions. New Moons provide all of us with clean slates to write a new script upon, if your Moon sign is in Libra look to write new programs about what you need, and ask for, in relationships.

Even if your Moon sign is not in Libra, you will still feel the effects of the New Moon in your emotional body. You'll also be given the change to plant new seeds of intention around the energy of Libra. Additionally, the combined power of both the Sun and the Moon in Libra supercharges this vibration and makes it available to all of us. It's as if we all become honorary Libras for this New Moon, feeling Libra's vibration in our entire energetic field.

We all have some piece of us that is governed by the energy of Libra. Our energy is defined in astrology by our natal chart. You can look yours up at astro-charts.com. Your natal chart is comprised of all twelve zodiac signs covering your twelve houses. Some of these houses have planets in them, some of them do not. Even if there are no planets in the house, you still have that house and governing sign, in your natal chart and your energy.

Houses can be complicated to learn at first, but they are the key to understanding how each New and Full Moon, as well as each Sun Season, will affect you. Houses represent areas in your life. Libra rules one of your twelve areas of life. This is the place that will be most affected by the New Moon in Libra. For instance, if Libra governs your tenth house of career, then you may want to focus on planting seeds around your workplace relations and partnerships. If Libra rules your third house of communication, you may want to write intentions around how you communicate to your partners on the New Moon. Your house governed by Libra is a great place to focus your New Moon intentions and explorations. You can always choose, however, to focus on a different area of your life than your Libra House. The New Moon energy can be applied anywhere you direct it, but looking at the house ruled by Libra can give you direction.

LIBRA X NEW MOON

This New Moon is all about creating balance and defining your relational space. We each have a number of relationships we embrace and invite into our lives. These can be with other people, with ourselves, with projects, ideas, and even time. The matrix of interconnected energies that comprise our relationships makes up our relational space. Just like any space, we have the power to define what, or who is allowed into this space, how much room they can take up, and how much attention we give to them. This New Moon brings us the opportunity to reorganize our relationships and ensure they are each serving our highest potential.

Libra brings us the element of air this New Moon, helping our mind move quickly and take inventory of what creates balance in our lives and what disturbs it. The first place to start this exploration is with yourself. What creates harmony within you and what disturbs it? Perhaps a person is distracting you from your true intentions, or a project is pulling your energy away from your focus on taking care of yourself. This New Moon is a time to release what limits your energy and replace it with things that expand it. If something, or someone, feels like a distraction or simply takes too much of your precious time and energy, then let the air element of this Moon sweep it away. When we take things off our plate, we open up space for new energies to come in, ones which hopefully will help us reach our highest intentions.

Before looking more deeply at your relationships with other people this New Moon, it's important to first look at your relationship with yourself. How you treat yourself and show up for yourself becomes the blueprint for all of your other relationships. For instance, if you don't support and believe in yourself to achieve your dreams, then you won't be able to attract people into your life who support you. Likewise, if you can not appreciate yourself for all that you are, then you won't attract people who appreciate your gifts and talents. A good place to start looking at your relationship with yourself is to take inventory of how you talk to yourself. We each carry conscious,

LIBRA X NEW MOON

and subconscious, mantras or sayings. Begin to look at the things you tell yourself daily. You can even write them down as they pop up throughout your day. Gather all of your common mantras and say them out loud. Are they hard to hear? Would you say them to anyone else? Hearing your mantras out loud can be a powerful exercise in understanding how you talk to yourself. We are often appalled at the things we automatically say to ourselves in the privacy of our mind. If this is true for you, how can you consciously replace your mantras with opposing words of kindness and compassion?

While you are looking at the relationship with yourself, consider your relationships with the energies and intentions you are calling into your life. If, for instance, you plant an intention around creating abundance each New Moon, look at your relationship with abundance. How do you define it? Do have any preexisting mantras which may block you from calling it in like "money is evil." An example would be if you are trying to call in the perfect relationship but have a mantra which tells you no relationship can ever be perfect. Feel into your emotions around each of your intentions and if you are blocking them with your relationship to that energy, then adjust it and change the frequency you are putting out into the world.

Once you have worked on your relationship with yourself, begin to feel into your relationships and partnerships outside of yourself. Do your relationships bring you harmony and support you on your life's journey? Do any of your relationships need to be balanced? Meaning are you giving more than receiving or vice versa? When we are in any relationship with another person, we are constantly exchanging energy with them. We are also taking on their frequency, and they are taking on ours. Think about the people in your life and especially the ones that are closest to you. Do you feel alive in their presence and full of energy, or do you feel drained? If someone is draining you that doesn't necessarily mean you need to cut them out of your life, it just means you may want to adjust your boundaries when you are around them, and perhaps not give so much of your energy freely.

Furthermore, look at the relationships that trigger you and elicit an emotional reaction. Most of the time, these relationships are merely mirroring some part of you that you need to accept and work on. Can you openly communicate with your partners when they trigger you? Not by showing up with blame or accusations, but can you be vulnerable and genuinely share pieces of your inner world with them? Remember, vulnerability is the key to empathy, the cornerstone of any relationship. Choose partners who you feel safe enough to be vulnerable with and share your emotions. When you can create an open and honest dialogue with another, then you create space for that person to help you become the best version of yourself.

Enjoy this New Moon, but truly feel into it and your relationships. It's an important time to understand how energetic interactions are affecting your conscious and subconscious mind. We connect to so much- people, our work, media, causes, projects, and beliefs. See this New Moon as an opportunity to understand your connections and how you can nurture them, balance them, or let them go of them with grace.

SETTING UP for MAGIC

Each zodiac sign carries inherent energy. With this energy comes colors, shapes, scents, and elements which match its vibration. For every New Moon, we want to incorporate as many of these frequencies as possible. While none of them are required to align with the energy of the New Moon, they do help reflect the energy. Think of it as placing energetic mirrors around the room that help amplify and direct the energy. Use your intuition to guide the choice and placement of objects. Resist the urge to overthink about where they belong. Let the crystals, in particular, choose their location; all you need to do is listen.

Pick a space that feels centered and stable either inside or outside. Imagine a white light creating the boundary of the circle and place candles, crystals, and other items within this boundary. Place a crystal, candle, or another piece of magic in the center to give structure to the circle. This is also where you can set up a crystal grid to help direct the energy further. If you are creating an altar, you can place it in the easterly corner to help call in the energy of new beginnings. Know that your attention and awareness of the energy available is the most important thing for working with it. You can practice the exercises in this workbook in any way you choose; you can practice alone, on a train, or in a group of people around a bonfire. Your willingness to open up, to look within, and expand your consciousness is the most essential piece to this day.

The other pieces for calling in and aligning with the energy of Libra are listed below. You can combine them in any way you like.

Colors: Pinks, Pastel purple, light green
Shapes: Hearts, infinity loop
Texture/Fabric: Cotton, linen
Scents: Juniper, anise, violet
Flowers: Tuberose, roses, orchids, gardenia

Incorporate all these elements as well in your circle. Use candles for fire, a room diffuser or spray for air, the crystals and flowers to represent Earth, and have some water in a metal bowl. Once you set up your circle, cleanse the space with sage or palo santo. After the circle is cleansed, smudge yourself and your friends before they enter the circle.

You can begin the circle by acknowledging everyone in the room. You can then continue to the yoga if you are practicing, and then the meditation. Once you feel the room is centered, begin to talk about the astrology of the night and what it means for each of you. If it is a larger circle, you may want to designate a talking stick or crystal to give to each guest while they speak. After you've shared your understandings, continue with the questions in the workbook and the journaling portion. After everyone has finished, talk again about your experiences with the energy and the revelations which may have occurred. You can share as little, or as much as you like with the group. Never feel obligated to speak, sometimes energies need time to develop before they are brought to the light of day. At this point, you may also pull some cards to help tune further into your intuitive guidance. You can use tarot cards, Goddess cards, animal medicine cards, or any other decks that may be in your toolkit.

Once you've finished the circle, close it by having everyone close their eyes, and meditate on what they are grateful for tonight and every night. You can even practice being grateful for things which haven't come your way yet. Gratitude will attract them to your energy and let the universe know you are ready to receive them. Enjoy this time to be with yourself, your heart, and your soul. Get to know yourself on a deeper level and allow your life to unfold another layer each New Moon.

cards pictured left: Dreamy Moon Cards by Annie Tarasova

Lessons from Libra:

- mastering balance requires understanding imbalance.

- harmony is a work in progress.

- to understand another person's perspective you must first understand your own.

- a true partner inspires you to be your best self.

- spirit daughter

NEW MOON QUESTIONS

The next pages are for you to open up to yourself and receive the answers your soul already knows. Take your time with each question and be as honest with yourself as possible. You can always return to the breath as a resting place. Answer these questions on the day or days around the New Moon. Trust the process.

1. What is the first clue your mind, body, or energy gives you when you are about to lose your emotional balance? What helps you restore this balance?

_____

_____

_____

_____

_____

_____

_____

_____

_____

_____

_____

_____

_____

_____

_____

_____

_____

_____

_____

2. How is the relationship with yourself mirrored in your relationships with other people?

_____

_____

_____

_____

_____

_____

_____

_____

_____

_____

_____

_____

_____

_____

_____

_____

_____

_____

_____

_____

_____

_____

_____

3. How does it feel to be in supportive relationships, with each person helping the other on their life's journey?

_____

_____

_____

_____

_____

_____

_____

_____

_____

_____

_____

_____

_____

_____

_____

_____

_____

_____

_____

_____

_____

_____

_____

_____

_____

4. How does it feel to be in a relationship which isn't supportive, and how can you bring balance to those relationships?

INTENTION SETTING

Now is the time to plant your intentions for this lunar cycle. Some of these intentions will come to fruition by the next Full Moon; others will come into your world over the next six months by the Full Moon in Libra in April 2020. Your intentions help you call in the vibrations you need to create your dreams. Some intentions will usher in new behaviors, while others will serendipitously bring you new experiences and encounters which will propel your path forward.

On the Libra New Moon, it's most beneficial to create intentions around your inner harmony and how to maintain, as well as your partnerships. These intentions can include envisioning the perfect match for your energy. They may include raising the vibration of the relationship with yourself. They can also include other qualities of Libra, such as creating new methods to keep calm in any situation.

Take a moment and create a scene in your mind. In this scene, all that you wish to call in is already yours. All you desire to change has already occurred. Do not worry about how you will get there or the list of to-dos needed to accomplish your goals. Just focus on the feeling of already living your dream. Know with every ounce of your being that it is already true; it already exists for you. Also, know that your intuition will lead you to this dream, not your logic.

Write in as much detail as possible, and write without limits. Just let your mind explore. Align with the energy of Libra to clarify your dreams. What does your envisioned life feel like? How does this dream make you feel? What emotions does it bring up? As you write, feel a sense of gratitude for what you are dreaming; thank the Universe for giving it to you and thank yourself for creating it. Gratitude always creates abundance.

AFFIRMATIONS

The New Moon is a powerful day to dive inward to your most hidden subconscious thoughts and patterns. In this space, you'll find the programs that are directing your life behind the scenes, most of the time, without you even knowing. You can look to the house in which this New Moon falls for you to find some guidance on which area of your life these mantras might show up. For instance, if Libra rules your 3rd house, look for programing around your communication. What do you tell yourself about these things daily? Below write down your old programming. These can be things like "I'll never be good enough" or "It's too hard," "I must try harder," or "I'm not capable." Then rewrite your old mantras into new ones which oppose and challenge the old ones. Repeat your new affirmations daily until the next New Moon. Repetition is the key to new programming.

Write your old affirmations.   Write your new affirmations.

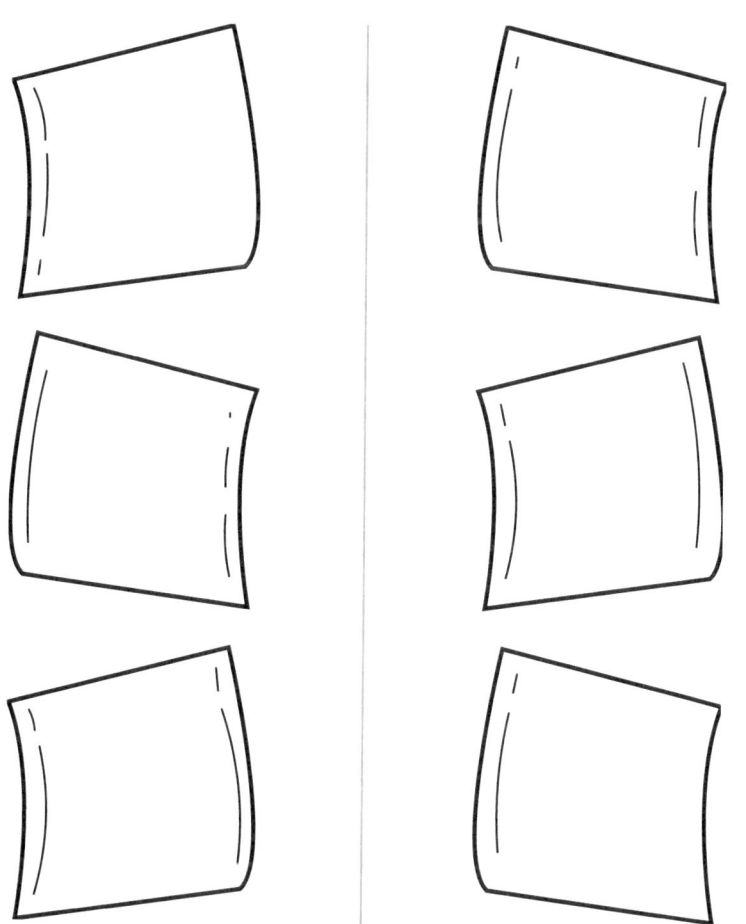

WAXING MOON

SEPT 29TH - OCT 12TH

BUILDING

Now is the time we build the foundation of our intentions as the Moon builds light. It is a time of action and also a time to watch for serendipity.

THIS WEEK I AM ATTRACTING:

_____

_____

_____

_____

_____

_____

THIS WEEK I AM EMBRACING:

_____

_____

_____

_____

_____

WAXING MOON

SEPT 29TH - OCT 12TH

TRANSITS

OCT 3RD: PLUTO DIRECT

Pluto stations direct, leaving his retrograde motion. Pluto teaches us to honor the cycles of our energy and transformation. Pluto asks us to embrace the process of change, even if it is uncomfortable.

What process, no matter how challenging, will help you transform?

OCT 3RD: MERCURY ENTERS SCORPIO

Mercury, the planet of communication, dives deep into the waters of Scorpio, bringing new depth to our internal and external conversations. Expect the hidden to surface during this transit. Also, expect communications to become a bit more intense and emotionally charged.

Mercury in Scorpio asks what is the underlying meaning of what you are saying to yourself and others?

OCT 4TH: MARS ENTERS LIBRA

Mars, the fiery planet of passion, enters the peaceful sign of Libra. Expect this transit to energize your relationships, either lighting them up or breaking them down. Mars in Libra helps us ensure that all of our partnerships are in line with our life's purpose and passion.

Do your relationships set you on fire, or do they dampen your flame?

OCT 8TH: VENUS ENTERS SCORPIO

Venus, the planet of love, enters the waters of Scorpio, intensifying our romantic relationships. Expect this transit to bring about transformative, in depth conversations and lots of cuddling afterward. Venus in Scorpio can bring out our obsessive nature, so be careful to take a break from your partners and give them room to breathe.

Venus in Scorpio asks how we can merge love and personal growth?

OCT 13TH FULL MOON IN ARIES

Please refer to the Full Moon Workbook for an in-depth explanation of this transit, along with practices and rituals.

WANING MOON

OCT 14TH - OCT 22ND

RELEASING & FORGIVING

WHAT I MASTERED THIS SEASON:

_____
_____
_____
_____
_____
_____

WHAT I WILL CONTINUE TO WORK ON:

_____
_____
_____
_____
_____
_____

WHAT I FORGAVE THIS SEASON:

_____
_____
_____
_____
_____
_____

✦ UP NEXT: ✦
FULL MOON IN ARIES
OCTOBER 13TH
IT'S TIME TO FIND YOUR POWER

Get ready to burn away what does not serve you.

AVAILABLE NOW!

HAPPY NEW MOON

———————

Thank you to everyone who supported and purchased this workbook.

Special Thanks to Rebecca Reitz (rebeccareitz.com, @becca_reitz) for her beautiful artwork on the cover, page 2, 10, 16, 32, 34.

For a monthly subscription contact hello@spiritdaughter.com or visit www.spiritdaughter.com. Follow along our journey IG: @spiritdaughter

Disclaimer: The exercises and yoga sequences in this book are physical activities that should be performed carefully to avoid injury. You agree to accept all risks and release Spirit Daughter and any guest instructors from any and all liabilities. Please take care and enjoy.